ICE AND THE EARTH

NIKKI BUNDEY

 Carolrhoda Books, Inc. / Minneapolis

First American edition published in 2001 by
Carolrhoda Books, Inc.

All the words that appear in **bold** type are explained
in the glossary that starts on page 30.

Lorna Delaney 11; Isabella Tree 29t / Hutchison Picture Library; Tony Page—cover
(inset) left / Jonathon Pimlott 13 / Pamla Toler 15t / Neil Morrison 23b / Ken Graham
25 / Impact Photos; Henry Ausloos—cover (background) / B & C Alexander 10,16 / R
Sorensen & J Olsen 12,15b / John Shaw 17, 20t, 24b / Hellio & Van Ingen 19 / Jean-
Louis Le Moigne 26t / Stephen Krasemann 27 / NHPA; Denis Bringard 4 / B & C
Alexander 6 / Roland Seitre 8b / Robert Henno 22 / Andy Crump 29b / Still Pictures;
cover (inset) right, title page, 21, 23t, 26b / The Stock Market; Streano/ Havens 5t / D
Burrows 5b / M Travers 7t / I Corse 7b / W Jacobs 8t / H Rogers 14 / A Kuznetsov 18 /
R Davies 20b / N Choat 24t / TRIP

Illustrations by Artistic License/Genny Haines, Tracy Fennell, Pete Roberts

Carolrhoda Books, Inc.
A division of Lerner Publishing Group
241 First Avenue North
Minneapolis, MN 55401 U.S.A.

Website address: www.lernerbooks.com

A ZOË BOOK

Copyright © 2000 Zoë Books Limited. Originally produced in 2000 by Zoë Books
Limited, Winchester, England

Library of Congress Cataloging-in-Publication Data

Bundey, Nikki, 1948–
    Ice and the earth / by Nikki Bundey
      p. cm. — (The science of weather)
    Includes index.
    Summary: Discusses the formation of various icy weather conditions and their
effects on the earth's surface, plants, animals, and climate.
      ISBN 1-57505-472-8 (lib. bdg. : alk. paper)
      1. Ice—Juvenile literature. [1. Ice. 2. Weather.] I. Title. II. Series: Bundey,
Nikki, 1948– The science of weather.
    GB2403.8.B86   2001
    551.31—dc21   00-027160

Printed in Italy by Grafedit SpA
Bound in the United States of America
1 2 3 4 5 6—OS—06 05 04 03 02 01

CONTENTS

Wintry Days	4
A Bite in the Air	6
Icy Climates	8
The Frost Factory	10
Icy Ground	12
Ice Crystals	14
The Deep Chill	16
Shaping the Land	18
Plant Survival	20
Animal Warmth	22
The Big Sleep	24
Fleeing the Cold	26
Ice Age or Heat Wave?	28
Glossary	30
Index	32

WINTRY DAYS

On a clear, cold winter's day, look out of your window. Roofs and yards are white and glistening. Puddles are frozen over, and **frost** covers the pavement.

Frost and snow are made up of tiny ice crystals. Ice is water that has frozen into a **solid**. Water can also be a **liquid**, like rain, or a **gas** called **water vapor**. Some places are icy all year long.

White frost covers the trees around a lake in a mountainous region of eastern France. The lake is partly frozen.

Ice is slippery and often smooth. It is difficult to grip. Snowmobiles like these in British Columbia, Canada, travel over the surface of the ice.

When the air **temperature** is below the **freezing point,** water vapor in the air freezes into tiny ice crystals. Icy weather takes many forms.

Snowflakes are ice crystals that fall from clouds. Ice crystals that form on the ground, plants, windows, and other surfaces are called frost. Freezing rain is rain that freezes when it touches cold surfaces. It sometimes forms an icy glaze.

Rain froze when it touched these branches. It formed a coating of ice.

A BITE IN THE AIR

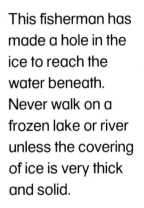

A layer of gases called the **atmosphere**, or air, surrounds the earth. We measure air temperature in units called **degrees**. One temperature scale is called Fahrenheit (F), and another is called Celsius (C). Water freezes at 32 degrees Fahrenheit, which equals 0 degrees Celsius.

Temperatures are measured with **thermometers**. These are usually glass tubes containing colored alcohol. Heat makes the alcohol **expand** and climb up the tube. Cold makes the alcohol **contract** and move down the tube.

This fisherman has made a hole in the ice to reach the water beneath. Never walk on a frozen lake or river unless the covering of ice is very thick and solid.

Falling water can freeze, forming long, pointed **icicles**. As the temperature rises, the icicles slowly melt back into water. The force of **gravity** pulls the water downward, causing drips.

As water freezes and turns into ice, it becomes lighter and expands, taking up more room. Because ice is lighter than water, a block of ice will float. As air temperatures drop, the ground gets very cold, too. Water in the soil turns to ice, making the ground rock-hard. A strong wind makes the air feel even colder. This effect is called **windchill**.

Ice floats in the ocean off the coast of Greenland. Seawater contains salt. Salt lowers the freezing point of water, so the ocean does not usually freeze, except in very cold places.

ICY CLIMATES

The typical weather conditions in a region over a long time are called **climate**. The coldest climates on earth are found in the **polar regions** of the Arctic and Antarctic. They receive less direct sunshine than regions around the middle of the world, near the equator.

Northern and southern regions of the world are usually coldest in winter. Winter comes to a region when its part of the earth tilts away from the warmth of the sun.

The top of Mount Cook in New Zealand is more than 12,000 feet above sea level. Heavy mountain snowfalls press down on the layers of snow beneath. The packed snow can turn into a **glacier**, or moving river of ice.

Antarctica is the coldest place on earth. A layer of ice up to three miles thick covers the ground. Temperatures can reach as low as −128 degrees Fahrenheit. Winters are very long there, and summers are short.

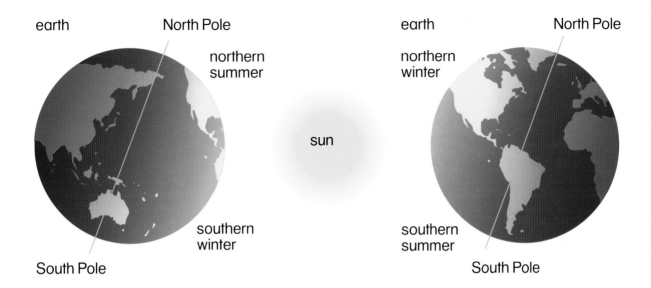

earth | North Pole
northern summer
southern winter
South Pole

sun

earth | North Pole
northern winter
southern summer
South Pole

Why do some parts of the earth have **seasons**? The planet tilts as it travels around the sun. As different regions tilt away from the sun, they become colder and experience winter.

Some parts of the earth are far from any warming winds or warm ocean waters. These places can be extremely cold. In a part of Russia called Siberia, temperatures can drop to –90 degrees Fahrenheit. The air is also very cold high in the atmosphere. Air temperature drops by about five degrees for each 1,000 feet that the land rises above **sea level.**

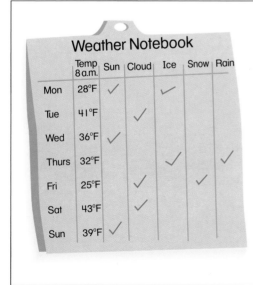

Weather Notebook

	Temp 8 a.m.	Sun	Cloud	Ice	Snow	Rain
Mon	28°F	✓		✓		
Tue	41°F		✓			
Wed	36°F	✓				
Thurs	32°F			✓		✓
Fri	25°F		✓	✓		
Sat	43°F		✓			
Sun	39°F	✓				

See for Yourself

- In a notebook, keep a record of cold weather conditions.
- Use a household thermometer to record winter temperatures at the same time each day.
- Note whether each day and night was cloudy or clear.
- Were the puddles, lakes, and rivers frozen over?
- Did frost cover the ground?
- Did snow fall?

THE FROST FACTORY

When the sun heats the earth's surface, liquid water in oceans and lakes may **evaporate**, turning into an invisible gas called water vapor. When the air holds as much water vapor as it can, we say it is **saturated**.

If the air cools, the water vapor **condenses**, turning into liquid **droplets**. They hang in the air, forming clouds, mist, or fog. In very cold conditions, ice crystals may form. Ice crystals that form high in the air may fall as snowflakes. Ice crystals that form on the ground are called frost.

As water vapor in the air cools and condenses, it forms mist or fog. Mist covers this reindeer herd at Verkhoyansk in Siberia.

Dewdrops hang from a spiderweb on a cold morning. Dew forms much as frost does but at higher temperatures.

When the sun goes down at night, the ground cools. Water vapor near the ground also cools and condenses. Water droplets called **dew** form on leaves and other cool surfaces.

The temperature at which water vapor turns to liquid water is called the **dew point**.

See for Yourself

How can you prove that air contains water vapor?

- Breathe out on a cold morning. The water vapor in your breath will condense, forming a little cloud.

- Breathe out onto a cold mirror or a windowpane. The water vapor condenses to form droplets on the surface, much like dew.

ICY GROUND

Sometimes, water vapor condenses into dew. If the surface holding the dew becomes colder, the dew will freeze, forming frost. Other times, frost forms when water vapor condenses directly into ice crystals instead of into dewdrops. This process occurs when the air temperature is lower than the freezing point. If the ground is very cold, it will soon cool the air above it.

On a clear night, the surface of the snow becomes cold and crisp. The snow **insulates** the soil beneath it.

12

Frost is most likely to form in clear, cold weather. Clouds act like a blanket around the earth, keeping the ground warm. When the sky is clear and cloudless, heat quickly escapes from the earth, and the ground becomes very cold. Frost often covers the ground on cold mornings in fall and winter.

Frost can coat grass and twigs with a thick white layer that looks like snow.

Frost is less likely to form in cloudy weather. The cloud layer insulates the earth's surface, keeping it warm.

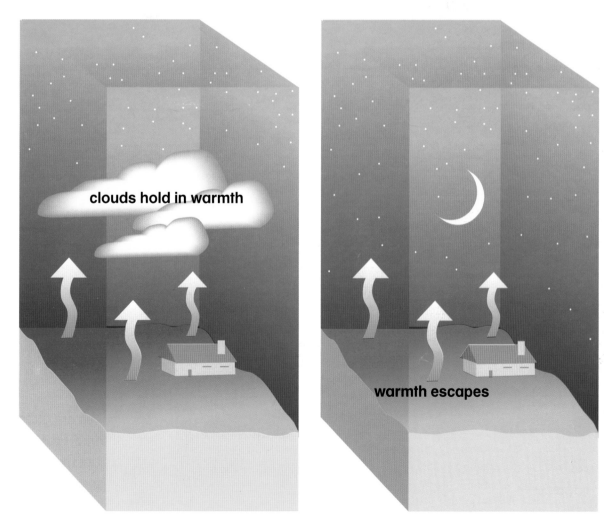

clouds hold in warmth

warmth escapes

ICE CRYSTALS

Water is made up of tiny parts called **molecules**. As liquid water cools toward the freezing point, its structure changes. Large spaces form between the water molecules. At the freezing point, the molecules come together in different patterns to form beautiful crystals.

If you look at ice crystals under a **microscope**, you will see that most of them are six-sided but that each has a different shape. The crystals may stick together to form snowflakes or frost.

Snowflakes are often star-shaped. Frost crystals are mostly needle-shaped or flat, like plates.

Layers of ice have formed inside a window.

As frost forms on cold surfaces, it often creates patterns that look like leaves or feathers.

When the temperature rises, the water molecules in the ice move closer together. Ice, frost, and snow melt back into liquid water.

On a very cold night, the water vapor you breathe out may condense into frost on the windowpane.

THE DEEP CHILL

The plains around the Arctic have such a harsh climate that few trees can grow there. These windswept plains are known as the **tundra**. Ice and snow cover them for most of the year.

During the short Arctic summer, only the ice crystals at the top of the ground melt. The ground beneath stays frozen and as hard as iron. This soil is called **permafrost**.

Snow and ice melt on the surface of the tundra during the summer. But the hard permafrost below prevents water from draining into the soil. Water lies in large pools called **meltwater**.

The water in the upper layer of the tundra's soil melts, or thaws, in the summer. The lower layer, called permafrost, stays frozen. This layer is often about 1,000 feet deep. In parts of Russia, it is more than 3,000 feet deep.

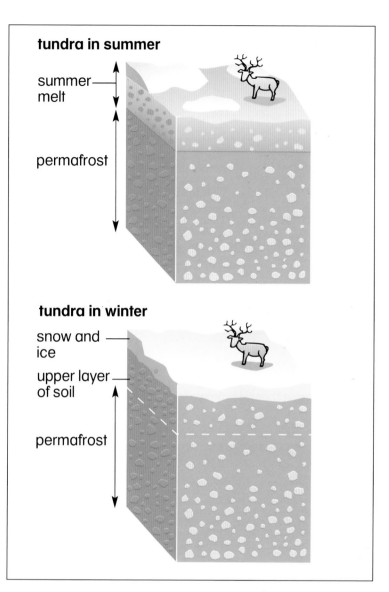

tundra in summer

summer melt

permafrost

tundra in winter

snow and ice

upper layer of soil

permafrost

Wildflowers spring to life during the short summer in Alaska. They root in the damp upper layers of soil.

The permafrost is like a giant freezer. It **preserves** the bodies of any animals that are buried in it. In warmer places, tiny living things called bacteria would make the bodies rot, but extreme cold keeps bacteria from growing in permafrost.

In Siberia, the permafrost has preserved the bodies of prehistoric mammoths for thousands of years.

SHAPING THE LAND

Water and weather conditions can wear down and shape the land. This process is called **erosion**. Glaciers dig out huge valleys. The ice grinds large boulders into smaller rocks and pebbles as it moves.

As wet soil freezes, the ice crystals in the soil expand and make the soil crumble. On farms and in gardens, the loose soil is easy to prepare for planting in spring. Farmers break up the soil with plows.

When water soaks into soil or rock, it may freeze and expand. It then melts and drains away, leaving cracks and holes in the rock.

Craters full of meltwater dot the Russian tundra.

On the tundra, freezing and thawing erodes the soil in different ways. The ice and water can push rocks into rings and other shapes. **Pingos** are created by pockets of water under the ground. The water freezes and expands, pushing up the ground to form mounds. When the water melts, a mound may collapse and form a crater full of meltwater.

See for Yourself

- Fill a plastic box with waterlogged soil.

- Put the box in a freezer.

- Remove the box when the soil is frozen. Does the frozen soil take up more room than the wet soil did?
- What is the soil like after it thaws out again?

PLANT SURVIVAL

Frost and ice are enemies of plant life. Plants soak up water through their roots and pass out water vapor through their leaves. This process is called **transpiration**. If the water in seedlings, shoots, buds, and leaves freezes and expands, plants might die.

Frost damage turns plants brown. They look as if fire has scorched them. Ice can weigh down stems and break them.

This cottonwood tree is in Yellowstone National Park. It survives harsh winters by shedding its leaves.

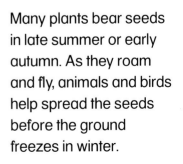

Many plants bear seeds in late summer or early autumn. As they roam and fly, animals and birds help spread the seeds before the ground freezes in winter.

Leaves fall to the forest floor when the autumn frosts arrive. The leaves provide a useful home for insects and other small creatures. The leaves slowly rot and enrich the soil.

In icy lands, trees have **adapted** to live through winter frosts. In cold places, water supplies may freeze for long periods. Spruce trees protect their seeds in woody cases called cones and grow tough needles instead of leaves. Oak trees shed their leaves in winter. Trees that shed their leaves are called **deciduous**.

In tropical countries, the climate is warm and wet. There are no frosts, so trees keep their leaves all year round.

ANIMAL WARMTH

In the freezing lands of the Arctic, birds are the most common form of animal life. Birds are **warm-blooded**, meaning they are able to make their own heat. Most **cold-blooded** creatures, such as snakes, cannot survive in very cold places.

Mammals are warm-blooded, too. They often have coats of fur or hair that thicken during the cold winter months. Mammals molt, or shed their extra fur, when spring comes.

Birds like this European robin fluff out their feathers in the cold. The feathers trap warm air and insulate the body. Oil on the feathers makes them **waterproof** and also helps keep the birds warm.

These Russian gray wolves have fur coats. At night they may dig holes in the ground for shelter. By day they keep warm by running. Food supplies their bodies with energy and warmth.

A layer of body fat is a very good insulator. It protects animals such as polar bears, which hunt on the ice and swim in Arctic seas. Many ocean creatures such as whales, walruses, and seals have thick layers of fat called blubber. Blubber keeps the animals warm.

A harbor seal swims among chunks of ice in the Arctic Ocean. A layer of fat protects seals against the cold. These animals also have a smooth coat of short, coarse hair.

THE BIG SLEEP

Some animals don't search for food in winter. Their bodies slow down for a few months, until they almost stop working and don't use much energy. This way of saving energy is called **hibernation**.

Snails are cold-blooded. Their bodies are made of mostly water, so a freeze would kill them. In winter, snails wedge themselves behind stones for shelter. They seal their shells with a chalky covering. This covering insulates snails' moist bodies.

Adders live farther north than any other snakes in Asia or Europe. They survive the winter by hibernating. Adders huddle together under logs for warmth.

The Arctic ground squirrel lives in Alaska and Canada. It hibernates for nine months of the year, insulated in a burrow. Its heartbeat slows down. The squirrel has reserves of fat but needs little food because it uses hardly any energy.

A sleepy Alaskan grizzly leaves its den for a winter snack. These large brown bears give birth to their young in their warm winter dens.

Some warm-blooded creatures hibernate, too. The name *dormouse* means "sleeping mouse." During winter, the dormouse curls up into a ball. Its body becomes stiff, and its temperature drops. It is very hungry when it wakes up in spring.

Bears do not truly hibernate, but many of them stay in their dens and become very drowsy in winter. The American black bear spends up to seven months of the year in this state.

FLEEING THE COLD

Winter's hard, icy ground makes finding food difficult for many kinds of birds. They cannot peck for worms in the soil. Food plants and insects die, so birds cannot eat them in winter.

Some birds **migrate** to look for food. Many geese fly north to the Arctic tundra in spring to feed on insects and grasses. Before the winter freeze begins, the birds fly south to warmer lands.

In summer, curlews live near freshwater. In winter, they migrate to **salt marshes** and beaches. Saltwater has a lower freezing point than freshwater, so the birds have a better chance of finding soft, unfrozen mud near saltwater. They use their long beaks to probe the mud for food.

When winter comes to the Canadian tundra, geese and their newly hatched youngsters head south. They fly to the warmer coasts of the United States.

Rocky Mountain bighorn sheep migrate up and down mountainsides. They spend winter on the warmer, lower slopes, below the **tree line**. In summer, as the snows melt, they head up to the higher slopes.

Some mammals migrate with the changing seasons. Herds of caribou take shelter in evergreen forests during the winter, and in spring they head north. They go to the open tundra of the Arctic, where the snow and ice are beginning to melt. The caribou have broad hooves that help them walk across snow, slush, and bogs.

See for Yourself

- Make a bird feeder for your yard in winter.
- Put suet, seeds, or stale bread in the feeder.
- Keep a record of all the birds that use your bird feeder.
- Use books to figure out which of these birds are winter visitors and which live in your area all year round.

ICE AGE OR HEAT WAVE?

The earth's climate does not always stay the same. During past **ice ages**, great sheets of ice stretched far beyond the polar regions. Sometimes, ocean currents, such as the Gulf Stream in the Atlantic Ocean, change direction. As a result, warm coastal areas freeze up. Most climate changes happen slowly, over thousands of years, but some happen more rapidly.

An artist gives us an idea of life during the last great ice age, when thick ice covered northern parts of the earth. Between about 9,000 and 15,000 years ago, the temperatures began to rise again. The ice started to melt.

An **iceberg** breaks away from the melting **ice shelf** and floats out to sea. Scientists who study Antarctica have found many signs of global warming. One sign is an increase in the number of flowering plants in Antarctica.

Scientists believe that the earth's climate is changing very quickly. World temperatures are rising. This process, called **global warming**, may be caused by **pollution**. Gases from car exhausts and smokestacks help to trap the sun's heat near the earth.

The Maldives are very low-lying islands in the Indian Ocean. They could disappear if global warming continues. Sea levels will rise as warmer temperatures melt polar ice. When the last ice age ended, the sea level rose by 427 feet.

Global warming could heat up icy and snowy areas of the world. It could also bring storms and fierce weather conditions to many regions. Scientists are working hard to learn about the causes of global warming.

GLOSSARY

adapted	Changed to survive in particular conditions
atmosphere	The layer of gases around a planet
climate	The typical weather in one place over a long period
cold-blooded	Having a body temperature that is the same as the temperature of the surroundings
condense	To turn from gas into liquid
contract	To shrink and take up less space
deciduous	Shedding leaves in winter
degree	A unit on a scale, such as those used to record temperatures
dew	Tiny drops created when water vapor condenses on cold surfaces
dew point	The temperature at which water vapor condenses
droplet	A tiny drop of water. Droplets join to form raindrops, hailstones, or snowflakes
erosion	The wearing down of the landscape by wind, water, or ice
evaporate	To turn from liquid into gas
expand	To grow bigger and take up more space
freezing point	The temperature at which water turns to ice (32°F)
frost	Ice crystals that form on the ground, plants, and other surfaces
gas	An airy substance that fills any space in which it is contained
glacier	A river of ice, made from compacted snow
global warming	The warming of the earth, possibly caused by air pollution
gravity	The force that pulls objects to earth
hibernation	Spending the winter in a drowsy, inactive state
ice age	A cold period in the earth's history
iceberg	A large mass of ice floating in the ocean
ice shelf	A broad, flat sheet of ice stretching out from the land into the ocean
icicle	A needle of ice formed by freezing drops of water
insulate	To prevent the loss of heat
liquid	A fluid substance, such as water
mammal	A warm-blooded animal that feeds on its mother's milk. Humans are mammals
meltwater	Water left behind after ice has melted

microscope	An instrument that makes tiny objects look larger
migrate	To travel at regular seasons in search of food or breeding grounds
molecules	Tiny particles that make up substances
molt	To shed fur, hair, or skin
permafrost	A deep layer of frozen soil that never melts
pingo	A mound created by pockets of water freezing in permafrost
polar regions	Areas around the earth's most northerly and southerly points
pollution	Poisoning of the air, land, or water
preserve	To keep from decaying
salt marshes	Flat land that is often flooded by saltwater
saturated	Holding as much liquid or vapor as possible
seasons	Winter, spring, summer, and fall, caused by the tilting of the earth
solid	A substance that has a specific form and shape, unlike liquid or gas
temperature	Warmth or coldness, measured in degrees
thermometer	An instrument used to measure temperature
transpiration	The process in which plants give out water vapor
tree line	The upper limit of tree growth on a mountainside
tundra	Treeless regions bordering polar ice
warm-blooded	Having a warm, constant body temperature, regardless of air temperature
waterproof	Able to keep out water
water vapor	The gas created when water evaporates
windchill	The cooling effect of the wind

INDEX

air, 5, 6, 7, 9, 10, 12
animals, 17, 20, 21, 22, 23, 24, 25, 26, 27
Antarctica, 8, 29
Arctic, 8, 16, 22, 23, 24, 26, 27
atmosphere, 6, 9

bacteria, 17
birds, 20, 22, 26, 27

climate 8, 16, 21, 28, 29
clouds, 10, 13
condensation, 10, 11, 12

dew, 11, 12
dew point, 11

energy, 23, 24
erosion, 18, 19
evaporation, 10

freezing point, 5, 6, 7, 12, 14, 26
frost, 4, 5, 10, 12, 13, 14, 15, 20, 21

glaciers, 8, 18
glaze, 5
global warming, 29
gravity, 7

hibernation, 24, 25

ice ages, 28, 29

icebergs, 29
ice crystals, 5, 10, 12, 14, 18
icicles, 7
insulation, 12, 13, 22, 23, 24

meltwater, 16, 19
migration, 26, 27
molecules, 14
mountains, 8, 27

oceans, 7, 23, 28, 29

permafrost, 16, 17
pingos, 19
plants, 17, 20, 21, 26, 29
polar regions, 8, 28
pollution, 29

soil, 16, 17, 18, 19, 21
summer, 8, 9, 16, 17, 27

temperature, 5, 6, 7, 8, 9, 11, 12, 15, 25, 28, 29
thermometers, 6, 9
transpiration, 20
trees, 16, 20, 21, 27
tundra, 16, 17, 19, 26

water, 4, 7, 10, 11, 14, 18
water vapor, 4, 10, 11, 12, 15
weather, 5, 8, 9, 13, 18, 29
windchill, 7
winter, 4, 8, 9, 13, 17, 20, 21, 24, 25, 26, 27